CARNEGIE-MELLON UNIVERSITY PRESS

P.O. BOX 21 CMU

PITTSBURGH, PA 15213

DREAMS BEFORE SLEEP

Poems By

T. Alan Broughton

September 15, 1982

$13.95 cloth

$ 5.95 paper

DISTRIBUTED BY

UNIVERSITY OF PITTSBURGH PRESS

127 N. BELLEFIELD AVE.

PITTSBURGH, PA 15260

Please send two copies of any
notice or review.

DREAMS BEFORE SLEEP

Books by T. Alan Broughton

Poetry

In the Face of Descent
Far From Home
Dreams Before Sleep

Prose

A Family Gathering
Winter Journey
The Horsemaster

DREAMS BEFORE SLEEP

Poems by

T. ALAN BROUGHTON

Carnegie-Mellon University Press

Pittsburgh 1982
Feffer and Simons, Inc., London

ACKNOWLEDGMENTS

Acknowledgment is made to editors of the
following magazines in which most of these
poems first appeared:

*AAUP Bulletin, Chowder Review, Commonweal,
Confrontation, Descant, Graham House Review,
Literary Review, Michigan Quarterly Review,
New England Review, Northeast, Poetry,
Poets On:, Southern Humanities Review,
Virginia Quarterly Review, West Branch,
and Yankee.*

The publication of this book is supported by grants
from the National Endowment for the Arts in Washington,
D. C., a Federal agency, and from the Pennsylvania
Council on the Arts.

Library of Congress Catalog Card Number 81-71589
ISBN 0-915604-68-X
ISBN 0-915604-69-8 pbk.

Printed and bound in the United States of America
First Edition

For Harriet Wilson: *godmother, bookgiver*

O sol che sani ogne vista turbata,
tu me contenti si quando tu solvi,
che, non men che saver, dubbiar m'aggrata.

Dante, *Inferno*, XI, ll. 91-93.

CONTENTS

IV   Traveling Together

V   The Lively Dead

I   A VICTIM OF MUSIC

INVOCATIONS

I laid a bowl of blood by the dark hole
and begged them out. They danced with me.
When they tired I grappled them down
and before they could curse me and retreat,
bound them, made them bleat their stories.

Their vengeance is silence.
They cried out to their friends
and now I wait, blood clots,
and when I call down, my own voice
dies without echo.

Too curious, they will come again,
cannot resist the light. I will try fruit,
freshly baked bread for them to imagine
eating. I will pretend to laugh
carelessly, prancing close to the rim.

I seize her by the hair,
not caring if her head is ugly
or her cries obscene. I hold her
mad face, kissing cracked lips until they calm.
Again I have you crone,
shift as you will. I am all of you,
all these tongues speaking for the lively dead.

WAKING THE DEAD

I pass a classroom
where someone is reading Yeats.
His tongue has a Bangor burr
telling out words that need no brogue.
Sometimes above me Milton is declaimed
and travels down the heating ducts
as I explain the last use of subjunctives.
We cling to our language here
though polyglotted blood is ours:
Jew, Italian, Slav, or African.

Somewhere across the quad
a class is using new techniques
to study Latin. They talk it,
groping to converse. Shyly she stands
and gestures at the glass. Beyond,
the sun has split the clouds,
blares shivering on an icy lawn.
"Ave," she says then finds her noun
for *light*, breaks into verbs.

Listen, the dead tongues stir
and rise to speak.

UTTERANCE

Beyond the curtain a woman moans.
I hear steel against steel,
the clip of scissors and casual talk of surgeon.
Humming softly to myself,
I wait for stitches.

I will be bustled in and out
and suffer stiffness for a day.
Worthless, she cries, *God damn, it's worthless,*
but repenting, *Forgive me, God.*
The doctor says, *At least I do.*
My numbed flesh absorbs the probe
that sews me back together.
I let her moans be mine.

That night I dream of reaching,
hands muffled in drapes.
The curtain falls across my face.
Tell me, tell me, I ask, but the cloth
assumes my shape and silence wears me.

I wake and walk lame through my house
already making up for lost blood.
Whatever wounds, the body strives to forgive.
Crows rattle in our spruce, trucks grind nearby,
and standing on grass where the axe slipped
I hear that woman breaking into voice,
give praise at least for waves of sound.

SONG

The empty birdfeeder hung on a knotted string
and swung against helical gusts of snow,
fooling chickadees perched on its rim.
When birds came back to sing in May
some warbler was drawn by a faint twitch
of last summer's luck.

In June when we return
no birds care. They sing dispersed
through neighboring hemlocks and fields.
We have deceived them too long,
leaving this husk for them to peck.
Trust us again, we say, filling it up.

I cannot bear woods empty of sound
and trick them for their singing,
wanting to stuff the trees with any notes,
even the nagging of bluejays.
I dream some hermit thrush, drawn
only by choirs of lesser birds,
will rise one evening to the tallest pine
and silence the woods with downward swirls.

Each morning I refill the cup,
lured by my need,
a victim of music.

REFRAIN

I start by listening to his song
and learn to need that red flash
when he rises to the spire
of Norway spruce and flutes at the sun
in its last roll of day.
Greedy for more, I buy a feeder.
This grows to trust.
He brings his mate.

They chip to each other in the maple
and flutter to ground. So courtly
he is, offering the best seed.
Our visitor who explained her divorce
sits by the window content
to watch that gash of air,
the crimson stain on green, green lawn.
They mate for life, she says.

This ends in the sickening of dismay.
The trashman comes and I assume
some bag has burst, leaking buff matter
on the drive. I start to sweep
but nothing can purge the eye
after it distinguishes feather, fluff,
a single twisted bone. My neighbor's cats
are somewhere in the shade, replete.

I find the sun too hot, retreat
to a cool house, my back to the windows.
But he sings. High in the spruce,
over a world of remains

he sends a voice down that has lost
none of its beauty, and in that cold retention
subdues the racked cries
of perishable claims.

TECTONICS

In sleep the continents drift back
to undivided shape. All night on thick limbs
I huddle and cling above the plain,
used to balancing in my dreams
where language is pure as fire.

But dawn is a question of light
before my eyes distinguish their confusion
in impossible slant of roofs or sharp bush
blazing with unnatural flowers.
Sun wakes a rolling world
and then displays the altered clocks.

I am in another land,
tongue numbed with ignorance.
Under my window a woman sings
as if she speaks for gulls,
mewing her syllables.
Someone calls out in the street,
a child shouts back. In anger,
or a warning of love?
The woman carries her song away.
Even the light must be translated.

BOOK BURNING

My son holds up his history text on Hannibal
who rides the cover brawny as Tarzan.
An elephant bears him angrily toward Rome.

He opens the sad remains.
Fifty pages in the center, a fistful ripped away,
edges burned, words charred.
I swerve back into lane, pulse hammering.
He hears me curse, shrugs to calm me down.
They're always doing that. I'll get them back.

His business, I keep saying to myself all day,
wanting to turn and bear that wreckage in hand,
a torch to burn their eyes.
The jerks in the back of the room have us again.
They do not descend with righteous vengeance
openly trumpeting some cause.
They hold their flames behind the desk and scoff.
Even their smirking faces look the same.

I will tell my son of bonfires,
of the lively sheen that burning books
cast on polished boots.
They are saluting, saluting,
jabbing stiff arms in each other's eyes.

II THE STILL CENTER

TO O'GRADY ON PAROS

Sea and sky are a field of seamless blues
and shade from an awning crosses your moving hand.
This is your home chosen from lands
you wandered through. You bring back words.
The poem begins again, and again you pause
to gaze past terraces, past spiraling gulls
to the faint shadow of a falling god,
wings melted in daring.

This is no Ithaca,
only another island where you rest
from migrations: Limerick, Alexandria, Boston, Rome--
an epic voice might list your passage,
and even at night sleep does not quiet the murmuring
in your mind of tongues that sing
for centuries of footloose bards.

You came to visit your landlocked friend,
a creature continental to the bone.
I keep a quiet shell, seas echo distantly
through my crooked chambers, and all I have
to offer is a narrow lake. Always we argue
even when we do not speak,
those loving confrontations of two ways.
I say, *A man to make an epic
stays at home*. You smile, translate
a fragment of Celtic lay, and suddenly
my wide country shrinks to an island
ocean torn.

That night, weary from traveling too long,
you dozed in spite of guests

carousing to your presence here.
How could we not see your death, old friend?
You did not conceal it. By evening you staggered,
groping for more wine with hands
that could not keep the shadows from your face.
When even this lurch and heave must stop,
I wish you in that place where obdurate land holds back
against the broken cries of ocean in the wind.

As host I tried to guard your sleep,
but someone randomly threw a folded plane.
We watched it loop, glide down, and land
in your lap. You did not wake.
For all the days left to me I will see
your quick hands lax, face numbed
and body at rest beneath those paper wings.

THE DISTANCE GOING NOWHERE

From the window he takes his last look.
Gray light is seeping back to the lake,
all trees and houses shape to snow.
Still it flutters down. One man
in topcoat and black hat wades slowly
through banks of fading white,
hands in his pockets, head down.
He crosses each pane of glass, balances
along the bannister, passes through posts
of porch and telephone. This ghost
is himself walking always
hands warm in his pockets,
or his father going somewhere impossible.
His grandfather too. One foot follows the other.
He puts his hands on the glass,
fingers spread.

FIRST SNOW, DEEP SLEEP, AS ALWAYS

He lights a fire, cups coffee
in his hands and sits by the window.
The cats perch on the sill
to watch birds at the feeder,
a squirrel below. The empty rooms
sometimes shudder with rising steam,
hisses the house makes against the cold.
He thinks this room, his figure in its chair,
the watchful cats, have been gently turned
by a giant hand, and down the glass ball
that surrounds them, white things
fall and fall.

AFTER GREAT PAIN

She knew how saints asked God
to shake them with His rough hand,
but she was only a mortal, fond
of bright fall leaf, yellow to yellow sun,
the craking geese wedging seasons apart.
Often she was bent double,
the world left her eyes
and in that dark enclosure
she cursed her long-loved flesh.
Later, watching rain churn by the street lamp,
dashing her window with flecks of light,
she would try to forget
how even Christ in the garden,
knowing what had to come,
found it almost impossible
to be human.

A BEND IN THE ROAD
FOR ROGER RATH

This evening I close myself in a car
and speed north past your town,
going nowhere, only as a way
to bring you back to mind.
I knew you slightly, touched by those wild
days of enjambment, speech whirling
from a mind blown high by its own velocity,
then utter silence where you watched
and nothing moved.

A summer wind lifts grass and leaves
as if a hidden fire burns under us.
The sun behind me glints on scales
of the Lamoille, its rapid turns,
then falls from the mirror. Ahead the moon rises,
and from porches of Johnson, lights are shining
on watchers and idlers, a figure hunching on the steps.
I could hear their low voices if I chose
to stop, but like you I will not,
driving into night until my headlights
flung on sharp pines and shattered rock
remind me of the consequence of drifting,
that halt of motion except
a wheel that spins in air.

I pull off on a dirt-edged curve,
the kind where battered road sign
warns with mute serpent, where an oil drum
lies and spews its trash.
I kill the engine, step into quiet
defined by a stream below, gusting wind
and distant rumble of jet.

Somewhere up the hill a car
begins its descent. The driver chooses
to accelerate in spite of the drop.
Headlights flash on rail and treetops,
I sense his panic in the cut-off engine,
shriek of brakes. He fishtails
into sight, blinds me with high beams
and is past, safe for home.
He has looked for a moment over the edge
and all the way down the long hill
his cold hands sweat.

I lean against this steel and glass
and stare into the place you left us,
that stillness at the center of all speed.

THANKSGIVING

Slouched in their cars,
redwool hats back on the head
and no bottle visible (but you know
it's there in the bulky vest
or slyly stashed between the thighs)
and guns in the back seat
or racked in the window,
they aren't hunting now
just sitting hardly talking
droop-eyed in the smoke
maybe having walked a field
and hoped that ten-point buck
would stand like a target,
here because home is a wife in angry curlers,
envy pinching her to a wince
and kids having found nothing
all day but buckshot words

and somewhere in the woods
high, where it's just begun
to snow (the first one, salting
the leaves with cracklings
you might take for flames
if you closed your eyes)
a buck is standing, head up
weight of horn not needed now
because he's already fought his way
to climb the hunched back

of a mate scarcely knowing
what was this sudden rub
that came long from his belly
and the standing thrust
that almost buckles her under him,
his neck down-curved
and snort drawn from a tightened body

and nose now to wind
he blinks at the snow,
will circle at dark
to try the last browned apples
where they cling, and by dawn
he will be haunch deep in snow,
wary of dogs.

WAR AGAIN

It is the war again
and we have gone to the beach
where dreams slide up the inner curl
of combers, night air takes their pulse
and mornings are still cool enough
for fiddlers to be unwary
and I am too young
to know more of time
than passage of meals,
the weight of naps,
my bucket and shovel and search
for unbroken shells.

But it is the war again and the sea
holds evil metal in its belly,
its eyes like lobster eyes
that see me as I walk the last
scud of foam, and once at night
we wake to watch the sky
streaked with bad veins of light,
the drone and ack-ack of static
through waves whose breaking
is phosphorous grins advancing.

And in the morning
all the beach is oily:
oil on my castle's wall

oil in the pool of sequestering
dabbled by crabs
oil on my feet and hands,
this rich earthblood that sticks.

It is the war again
and I am afraid,
shot down

the water burns
and how will I wash off
so much black?

FROM PURGATORY
e quindi uscimmo a riveder le stelle

Beyond an open door I see your back
straight as a chair. The wall you face
is unblemished in its gloss.
I talk, you blink. Once you unfold
your hands. Light echoes wall to wall.
Who guides you through those gates
downward, circle by circle to the frozen wind?
We wait for you here on the other side.
Do not forget your body still has weight.
Before I leave I touch your cheek
but silence turns my hand to shadow.
Others like me glide down
bearing quiet to the waiting room.
I pass the narrow door, breathe in the bitter air.
Look, I want to cry out to your wall,
the stars still shine,
as sane as they ever were.

FLOWERS FOR ELIZABETH

All I can do is bring
a gathering of blossoms,
whatever is in season,
chrysanthemums or marigolds,
offset them with a wreath of mottled leaves.
You have left us
with these gestures, old ways
of passing something to the place
where you are shut away.
We know better what we hold
than where you are.

I will keep this simple
as my love, will keep these words as plain
as the life you chose,
but will not accept that baroque growth of cells
that utterly slowed your swift body.

I hold each flower to you
one by one.

Your daughters,
restless as the fall wind
on the night you died.
One ate an apple
and wrote her name
over and over in cursive.
The other took her shoes off,
put them on and sometimes went out
to swing above the lawn.
Perhaps we should worry more

about the sons who were sleeping.
We could not see their dreams.

Your husband, hunched in a chair
by the window, and father who stood
and caressed his back.
They are still trying to accept
how when you woke that morning
you did not know them.

Your mother who talked
and leaned on any part of the room
but never sat down.
She spoke of her home in Florida
and the mercy of death.

I tell you a single rap on the door
woke me in the early morning
but I turned away to dream
you had come running, knocking
on all our doors once
to tell us you were gone.
You could not pause to enter--

so many doors to touch,
too little breath left.

I add small buds not unfurled
to fill this out:
a ragged sky,
clouds leveling the hills,
brooks in a tumble
as if it were spring. But that season
is yet to be earned.

I will not let this gathering
slip through my hands
as you did when I left your house
and you were dying.
By the time I reached my room
they called to tell me you were
dead.

I hold this out formally
like a torch,
thrusting it before me
as I try to see beyond
into the room you have entered.
But the light of memory

is too great, blinding
my eyes and they become merely
dark seeing the dark.

I drop these flowers here,
stems bent by the tight grip of my hand.

They fall away.
You have them now.
The room is closed.

ACCRETIONS

A parson's modest cabin displaced some trees.
After him summer people floated in,
scattering nooks with bric-a-brac.
The family before us ambled away
in sunny neglect--beds made,
a cookbook open near the sink,
pages gnawed to fill a nest.
I sleep on their initials, pricked
in the embroidery of sheets.

Five years ago we added our confusion,
pushing out the kitchen wall
until it leaned against the largest pine
and now when fall winds blow, the whole house
cracks and teeters, a wreck impaled on reefs
deep under the restless surface of the day.

Tonight I spread the coals
before I stumble to our bed.
Kneeling I count thirty years
feeding cracked bricks of that hearth,
shoveling away the ashes of dead flames.
I spin with outstretched hands

past wives and children, lovers
furtively pulled through woods while parents slept,
or dreams that flung me into seamless dark.

Over my head the chimney, stepped and wrung
to fit the corner of this room,
corkscrews into blackened rafters.
One dull knock under my feet
warns that a stone this summer
has fallen out of place. The porcupine
tucking a blunt nose to his tail
curls toward a long, neglectful sleep.

III   WORKS OF LOVE

TWO WORKS OF LOVE

I VILLA BORGHESE

The god's touch
turns her to
tree
　　　the virgin leaves
and branches starting
from below in
bright marble
frozen
　　　they
twist and cannot
fade
　　　but he
wears her only
on his head in
wreaths
　　　as Bernini
straining at his rock
also must have known
abnegation of
a Daphne shrouding
his hips in leaves.

II VILLA GIULIA

They lie and smile out
side by side being
so very terra cotta
rude in shape
with beauty in
their eyes
         much less
for us to see
than kindly mock-ups
for the gods
         made less
for fixed and high
intensity than by a
common hand
         who sensed
a couple's better
life when guards go home
and she turns to him
clay robes fall
and ornamenting
awkwardly each other's
flesh she opens
her imperfect lips
to him
         and all
the art they have
is art of living.

PHOTOGRAPHED ALL OVER

            In Paris
I was hunched to tie
      a shoe
she was about to bite
      an apple
                  in Avignon
I was avoiding
      a small man
                  bearing flowers
only her foot showed

            gradually
pursued down the boot
we filled in casual
            poses all the back-
and sidegrounds of
                  their snapshots

I mean all
            of them
Japanese and Argentinians
                        gay
businessmen from Fayetteville
a semi-retired orthodontist
            from Brazil
                        and they bore us
back to be developed
            blown up
                  shown
to friends as passersby

before the larger loved ones
          of the world
                         its
Notres Dames
                  and Big Bens
to give them scale
but we are invisible
to them
as if we'd never been there
she and I bent
                    to each other
having passed a year
in our own space
                    not seeing
them either

          no one puts all
the photographs together.

VISIT TO RUINS

Nothing endures like Roman brickwork
or the broken words of self-flattery.
Reticulate as the insect's eye
our own day pieced itself out
through uneven streets as we stepped over walls
to tread on bedrooms, making lizards uneasy.

No longer held by altars, the sun
began to set behind the autostrada,
one plane drifted up from Da Vinci
and I was too young to wake in such a place,
petulant with anger to be once more
in the jumbled way of intangible structure,
ruined maze of the tufa heart.

Now when we make love
and open our eyes face to face
I stare into the fullest coming:
an orange sun stretched out
in blank sky, our faces passing
on a black volcanic road, straying
without guidebook in some ancient port.

HELENE

I MYKONOS

The sea is bloodied by a slaughter house.
Through its doorway I glimpse the shorn ewe
struggling without voice, throat slit.
I show you the long trail of flux
seeping out with the tide.
This makes you angry.

In our lobby a doll sits in pink dress,
her black hair curled and arms held out.
That night on the way to bed
I turn her to the wall.

At dawn from the balcony I watch
a man on the distant pier,
arm lifting and falling in strict cadence.
He is beating a squid on the rock
but no sound arrives.

You lie in a tight curve under the sheet.
I cannot hear us falling apart.

II   KYKLADES IN FEBRUARY

We walk the streets of Naoussa
where gods become children again
ambling on cobblestones.
A girl with Athene's eyes, a boy
who wears some daimon's mask
are on their way to school, hand in hand.
What did he say? you ask.
He was only talking to the girl.
Wind scours, no respite from its moan
even in the center of a house.
White ocean tilts on its side
and in the farmyard a drunken helper
waves his arms, loose as the tattered windmills.
The air is filled with bells of sheep
but no one can find them.
Stalking each other jaw-clenched,
men loosen only under wine.

When the wind stops, the sea lies down
and in silence we walk again
to a peeled shrine on the rocks.
You watch the sea draw back from a cave.
Everything is more distant than possible.
That night you dream of the wild fig tree,
willing, the stranger's delight.

III   CEREMONY OF PARTING

I wake this morning and turn
to hover above your sleeping curve.
One of us will leave soon,
Vienna or maybe Rome.
Will I wave you off in a shrilling jet
or watch you turn once
at the corner of a twisted street?

Ithaca passes at night,
a wandering boy on deck blows his harmonica,
and this morning I can think of nothing
but the garden of your home,
your corn-yellow hair coiled down a white dress,
and how a long soft wind rose from the ground
fluttering all leaves up before rain
when we were married.

We are slipping backwards
on ocean dragged by the moon.
You lean on your elbows at the rail
and I sleep again, to wake
to your touch on my shoulder as you rise.
Some singer tells us
how beautiful is Rome in spring

while a man dances slowly with himself,
eyes closed and one hand on his chest.
The bloodorange moon slides into the sea
and the stranger beckons you over.
His hand on your hip
is a wing that comes to rest
and you smile at the sky beyond his head.
Slowly you are dancing out of sight.

HIC AMOR HAEC PATRIA EST

Why do they call it choosing?
I do not deny the countertug, the glance
back over my shoulder
and last voice saying, *Stop,*
it is enough only to know her
in the seasons of each day,
exploring the land where her shadow falls.

But I gather my life around me
and go down to the ship
where they wait to cast off,
and I stand looking long at her eyes
blue as the rim of evening sky,
her hand tight-knuckled on the rope--
always to be looking past her fading face
toward some whole music I faintly hear,
scored on a river's flow.

HAZARDS

Green folds of Devon toppled into jags of rock,
cathedrals were piled like cairns
on roads that straggled into moor or fen
or left us clinging to each other at Land's End,
fog deep in our throats.
We stood on a Roman wall
railing at cold rain, sentinels
to some grief that never attacked.
I had always traveled alone,
but no matter where we dropped to sleep
letting our hands go lax--
even if geese cackled us up at dawn
or bells brayed in unfamiliar tongues--
our bodies moved as if one pilot
steered them on. Now we are home
and drive our separate routes to work.
I am less vigilant for loss,
too often wake drifting down
the wrong side of the road.

SHIFTING LANDSCAPES

Dry leaves eddy by the door.
The lake will not lie down to ice
until the cold air holds,
pressing gray sky on a stoney place.
But I evade this scene to recall
another fall I walked in Alban hills
past cellars where last oozings of grapes
were foaming in the vat, where vinegar
filled the cracks of cobblestones.
Slowly I climbed the streets of afternoon
into a sun that wrung from bay and oak
the sweet acuity of green decay.
In the moss of old steps lizards clung
and blinked their slow watch.
I stood in long shadows to look down
on Lake Albano, turquoise in its perfect crater,
flecked by the last turnings of the day.
A dog was hunting the woods below,
baying at his own reflected voice.
Closing my eyes I saw this rocky place,
its long gash of water, more clearly
than if I leaned on my doorjamb.

LANDSCAPE WITH VANISHING POINT

She was everywhere I looked
but nowhere to be seen.
I pedaled for miles, braked
by jerks down woody curves
and wet my shoes at the ford.
Such distance was forbidden,
too far from home's safe linkage of voices.
I pumped and pumped
through sweat or rain or dust
of shattered leaf. Tipped over
I skinned my knees
and once a dog drew blood.

She should have risen naked from the weeds,
burdocks in her hair.
She should have turned her belly
silvered with bubbles in upstream pools
or clung by bare legs, about to plummet
from that apple by the bend.
But under the boughs the front wheel
spun on its side as I knelt
in nothing but fruit.

At last I found pressed grass
where she had lain, and signs

she kept no faith.
Before I left that place,
before speed flung me past
all hope of simple touch,
I stood on a hillside falling into the sun.
She swam across a field through wheat,
a single maple, flocks of crows.

LES NYMPHEAS

We walked in the lacquer glow of evening
past water, drowned leaves, floating sky.
I said, *That's like Monet.* But no part of France
saw such New England light, water
preparing to thicken into stone.
Yes, was her reply for more than art.
Our fall was wordless with excess,
with winded cries, even as snow fell
on her upturned face.

I always return to Monet.
Years of staring as if in prayer
are layered in confusion when I pause
before a waterlily. That old man,
portly with his cane, a face concealed
by broad-rimmed hat and beard
would not stop feasting on light.

But her face has dissolved.
That simple act so often repeated
with other women in other places
bears no imprint of our gestures
in sky, leaves, water.

A SEASON OF DREAMS

I   NIGHTMARE

Broken out of a sleep of quartz,
my own heart knocking at my chest
I grope across a room
lumped with encumbrances.

You stand in whatever light
the scoured stars give,
one fist held up to strike again.
Dark is a falling comber
closing over the street,
the listless house.

Your mouth frames words,
your hand unknots,
but air sucked under by the wave
rips the door from my clasp
and slams it between us.
I cannot leave the place
you might have entered.

II   THAW

In spite of mid-winter, air is risen
from fires; we live in a babble of warm winds
flapping me this way and that
and I tug against the fixed ends of my age.
All night I roll in the greenest grass
while you sit in a nearby tree
laughing at something, pointing away.
Come down, I call, *the grass is fine,*
but you look beyond me.

I wake in a buffeted dark,
certain I hear your voice
outside my window. Someone's wooden chimes
speak for the wind. I do not doubt
my urge is the unacceptable yammer
of bones that will never be still,
but cannot forget how it is to float
on the first touch of any bare clasp.

The slats of my cage are rattling,
so loose I could brush them aside.

III FANTASY

I imagine a room without windows.
I put you in it,
take off your clothes,
ask you to dress again,
tell you to be at ease.

You ask for windows.
I have carpenters come
from the best of the cities,
believing they know their business.
The walls are hardly damaged.

After the rasping, after the cleaning up
you notice there is no glass.
In fall sounds of crickets enter the room
all night, but you do not complain.

With the coming of snow
you no longer undress.
We nail sheets across the windows.
I ask you to dance
but you say, *Three's company*.

How we endure until spring
I will never understand.
I recall how red your knuckles became
and grease never washed off the plates.
I have two dreams

and forget them both
but you never complain.

When spring comes I find
your slippers by the window.
The tattered sheets flutter
like my hands. When I pull them down
I can see a landscape
you painted on the building opposite:
two apple trees in bloom,
a bear drinking from a tilted pail.

I hold one slipper to my ear
and hear the sea.

LOSERS, FINDERS

I drive the long way home
past fields and wooded curves
made twice as unfamiliar by wet snow
and drifts of fog.
When night drains the sky
I cannot conjure the shape
of my house approached this way.
The road dips, shrugs off
the last vestige of memory.
In fear I pump more speed
but only drive the unknown
closer to my face. Each light ahead
I make believe is home.
Could that pale and sunken lamp
be mine? Is that our maple
hunched by a ragged ditch?
The next house has no lights
but I slue up the drive,
walk each step slowly
so I will never forget again,
hoping beyond that door to find
the semblance of my life.

SYNECDOCHE IN WINTER

The sharp wedge of my neighbor's roof
holds back light, barely shifts
against a sun that hugs horizons.
Even my shadow is lean
and pale before the latent snow.

I still defend my portion,
and spruce, briar, sharp-winged jay
cut patterns on the ground.
The sun itself is fragment
of a burst that blasted light
into boundless separations, and night
is the turn to lie in our own shadow.

Before I sleep I watch the snow
reflect a reflecting moon,
each blocked or broken shape in that dim field
persisting in its reference to wholeness.

LAST MOMENTS

My life waits in the idling car.
I walk from room to room, closing each door behind me.
Floors are swept, windows nailed shut.
I check the stove, unplug a lamp
and pause in a living room
made fit to be a morgue.
Mice already scatter through walls
to practice their gnawing on the joists.
Even the air smells derelict.
We have not left, I think defiantly,
watch the warped panes twist
the languid motions of white pine.

My father must have stood like this
when I sat eagerly outside
only aware of picnics and cabins,
in love with forward time.
Now I stand where sun will not touch
till spring, and cold seeps up from stones
reclaiming the sagging floor.
My mind walks backward through every room.
All doors open behind me,
lintels collapse like unsinewed bone
till even rock, tree, bare sun
are waiting to return.

AURORA

None of us in that room spoke
as if each was part of his own dream.
I would not eat the food. Wide stairs
were walked by lines of hooded figures.
The hand that took mine, face
that still did not speak
had never come to me before.
We walked the narrowing stairs
worn by centuries of passage,
until the tower turned to wood.
No railings held me back. The catwalk
swayed as her feet spiraled into light.
I crouched away from the plummet
while birds beat in anger at my head,
and woke in an unknown dark
to gather knowledge slowly.

A campfire smoked.

The ground was cold. Some trees were flailing
at the stars. Untangling my body,
I walked into the clearing far from any city
of my dreams. The sky shivered with light.
I watched that hard fire peak and die
then lay down by your side again,
and this was only one night
of our lives together.

SILENT LIGHT

A heave of light,
explosion no one hears
thrusts outward making space.
I learn the diagrams,
hear ticking blurred by billions of years,
and even tonight stand on my porch
looking at stars whose present light
I'll never see.

I cannot live without
diminishment of sound.
Wind shakes the house. I wake.
A siren twists through town.
Revelations are quiet
as if that road I walk so often,
bent by the brook and torn each year
to grit that looks the same,
suddenly burns with a bush, a voice
that only one mind hears.

My dream this night
showed me a field I stumbled through
knowing you were never born
but searching you through high wheat anyway.
I turn and place my palm on your arm,
rush forward with the rhythm of your breath.

IV TRAVELING TOGETHER

AGAINST LAMENTING

You tumble apples into the trough, I shred
and they roll their white-shocked flesh.
Sometimes October showers pock
the rising cider in its barrel,
or sun steams the bare wet limbs.
Our labor keeps us warm.

When I screw down on pulp
foam churns over the platen
and even the handle grows sticky.
Once I plunge my arms deep in the vat
to retrieve an apple. None escapes
the fury of our cranking.

The books I read this morning were clad in gray.
Poems tolled to me across wide plains--
high, pale tones carried on lapsing winds.
Even pain buzzed and fell like a fly
fumbling to get out, disconnected
from bright worlds beyond clear glass.

Wasps crawl over the brim,
 long legs slowed by nights of frost.
They drown to drink that sweet, dark water.
We'll lug it in, fill carboys,

let the magic of fermentation boil it
into pale wine, the spirit of apples.

But now, in the last quick slant of sun,
we do not waste the mounds of foam.
We dip our hands, eat from bowls of flesh
and kneel for more.

JANUARY THAW

I'll be your goat man,
hairy-thighed springer,
drink only retsina tonight.
Give me the pine-pitched dregs
while I weave upstairs,
nudging walls and toppling
a table in the hall.

Who cares if the madame shrieks—
we've locked the door
and I'm already bare to the haunch.
We'll wobble into an old brass bed
and roll till the plaster cracks,
and oh, my sweet, you're better
than the best ewe of the flock.
Then I'll sleep and sleep
like honey stored in a dark hollow
of the oldest olive, high,
high over the Bay of Corinth.

A SLANT OF LIGHT

I return from a jabber of clocks and cash.
As we walk to the river, you gather our world
with gestures, pointing to elderberry,
its candelabras bending and purple.

You grip my arm, we cannot speak
as a great blue heron spreads upward,
slow as held breath.
He flies into a sun wedged between
the hard lined cloud and ridge of earth.

Each brittle bush and weed,
the smallest stones at our feet
are hewn by light so fierce
that lips are dumb with love.

ARIA DA CAPO

I feared the same sun rising
day after day to unchanged eyes
and framed by a constant window.
How could I bear the vision
of a single tree, rooted in the monotony
of a plot no plantings could rearrange?

So I moved, taking my eyes with me.
Each window for a time seemed new,
and that trickery of sight altered
the shape of sky, if not the sun.
But nothing I formed with my hands
remained in view--the planted bush,
barely worn haft of an axe or sledge
were backwards in time, and I stared
always ahead.
               But here, love,
I wait each afternoon for your return
and lie down in the bed you make each morning.
I rise to see dawn in its framework of drawn blinds
and raising them, watch a moon descend
into unvarying lines of hills,
the rock-bound shape of quivering lake.

I hunger to touch again and again
the tools that hold this house together

and I am a glutton for seasons,
keeping a journal of our sun's small variations.
Each night I pray for repetition--
to wake as the same branched shadows
shake the brightening air.

A MIDSUMMER'S DAY DREAM

How simple. As easy
as waking from long sleep.
Windows are open, the sun
as always in this season drifts
through softening layers of air and branch
to slow shuttling on the shadowed wall.
I can wear those patterns on my hand.

Wake slowly with me, love.
So often I have risen abruptly,
heaved on my clothes, slammed doors
and crossed this clearing blind.
The last dream shoved me
with rough hands toward the next
and I clung shivering to my ignorance.

Slowly, my love. Remember how simple it is—
my body entering yours, our eyes widened
to take in light on each other's face.
The day is long, and we can walk
its pace, passing without harm
over the summer's loam, down to the brook
to admire that clarity of motion not our own.

And later, even the shortest night
is long enough to fill
with all our lives.

SOMETIMES SUCCESS

All day you glued and painted.
Chips of plastic, strips of decals
littered the floor. Once your knife slipped,
gouging through veneer.
Even upstairs the air was stained
with turpentine and faint whiffs of ether.

You took me to a field
to watch the rocket of your labor.
Sun strove to bring green
out of Easter grass, other children
flew their kites, a flutter of plastic
that swooped infallibly to trees.

You counted down. The red light
of your launcher blinked, you pressed,
a straight-edge ripped the air past kites
and gulls swerving on mere wings.
And paused. In silence,
in puzzled drift, it hung,

wobbled into a plummet, tumbling
frail wood and cardboard, spent.
You ran, wind freshened, blew it
away from us, but with a pop

long strings unwound.
A parachute puffed out its scarlet stripes.

You stood with hands in pockets
watching your plans come safely down to earth.

FALL GAMES

I hold a rake on the lawn,
you lean against the barrow.
We stare at the sun through leaves
that have to fall.
You are twelve and eager
to heap them in piles,
make one last leap. *Next year,*
you say, *I'll be too old for that.*

Wind shakes the boughs,
leaves break loose
and stain the air.
You hold out your hands
and run. I drop the rake
joining your wild attempt
to catch these dizzy colors.
We lurch through maple
and reluctant oak.

WAKING OLDER

When I was five you sang
That Old Black Magic and during the day
I baited a hook with balls of bread,
dangled my legs above the lean-eyed gar,
slant shadows of fear. The snake boy
was a mute who smiled
and held up snails and tadpoles
to my face. Safe in our rented rooms
I heard storms hammer that lake,
and then your voice would tuck me
into amphibious dreams.
You took me to the sun
for health, and what I carried away
was an image of shelter, the quiet
between the breaking of each wave.

SLOW MOTION

I GOING TOGETHER

We leave the curb
too fast for Mother's liking,
but I am impatient to pass the duckpond
where I threw stale bread,
hoping to lose my way.
On the edge of remembrance
I lean through that turn in the road
where once a piston kept us from going.

Father recalls the time a dog leaped
and he swerved, but Mother says
that was before I was born.
When I stop kicking the back of the seat
Grandmother sinks into other years
and I slump toward the rapid tires
humming, humming.

On the last hill the key is turned into silence,
we glide with only a wind of passage
heard deep in the blood.
The wheels slow, we lean forward,
and into the valley of darkness
all the generations in one car
are coasting, coasting.

II LULLABY

Be careful, you mutter,
sluffing your body onto my shoulder
to loll in trusting sleep,
further from home than either of us wants.
The wheel lets me believe that I control
cars swerving back into lane.
My dimmed lights fall on unfamiliar ground.
Hell may be a landscape without stars
but I've no time to gaze at sky,
and anyway this seems no less than earth,
as simply repeating my ignorance of it
as ever—trees rushing at me, fields
thrust at a tilt, a sudden mountain
heaped like a swarm of cloud.

Two bridges left to cross.
Slowing I hear crickets, then stop
to watch the stars move on.
Wake, son, to a moment blurred with doubt.
Where are we, where is our ceaseless rush?
Wake to a world that holds you,
full of care.

III PERPETUAL

I thought myself the quick
driving through shifting leaves,
rising six tiers to stand at your bedside
and watch you fold me in
with slow, grave eyes.
How many childhood fevers you led me through,
the shadow of a father bent
to hand me up the steep bank of bad dreams.

You say we drove last night
to places I could never know.
a dirt road twisting by farms
falling the long hill to your family's own.
You put me at the wheel,
gripped my shoulder as I shifted down,
slued into the yard to stop
in our dust in time.
Your parents waited there,
lamps lit, their silent faces pale
as marble gods turned to the unlatched door.

Before you woke you trudged back
through the long valley of pain.
Now I will drive us to our steps,
then let your weight lean into mine.
Traveling together,
we almost seem at rest.

V   THE LIVELY DEAD

SHE DREAMS A WAY

I.
Doctor,
I do not lose weight.
All your chairs sigh under me.
But I have come to tell you
about my dreams,
the lean as well as the fat.
I am still husked in my flesh
but a new soul grows there.
I am coming unfurled.

II.
This starts in a room like a grave
where without need they are burning
the useful things:
someone's glasses, perfectly good
shoes, a Persian rug,
my mother's afghan.
How do I get out
of this stench?

The door slams behind me
on a windless day.
I am left with the stairs
but they are unfinished.
So many rooms to the left
or the right and all unfurnished.
I make my own risers
and plant a chair, a table,
a divan. I am up to the attic
and pry at the split in the roof
with clawed hands.
The furniture needs water
to grow.

III.
I enter a land
of flowers I have never seen.
I know all stalks
and trees elsewhere.
I shout on the lawn
I tell you I can classify
all other plants.

These flowers are hollow.
My voice enters them
and does not come out.

IV.
Please keep my feet dry.
I half wake and pull them up
close to me. Is it this fat
that slows my blood?
I hate wet feet.
The bridge begins to sink
like a waterlogged plank.
The waves mock and are hungry.

But when they touch me
my breasts grow stiff,
no longer hung or swinging
from a swollen body.
My lips open and close
and are their own caressing.
I ride my waves
and wake to my honied
moans and cries.

V.
How sweet to give
something away
that you have always wanted.
A great light shimmers down
and white surrounds me.
I am lean as a flame.

VI.
I wake in the temple
near the shore where
the white birds always hover
and tune the sky.
What columns and friezes,
how scrolled and volute
is this stone.

There is a boat
with a single white horse
beyond the fringed turnings of waves
and I am clothed in blue veils.
I will ride that horse someday
far into the land.

On all the cornices are
blue birds I have seen nowhere
but in my dreams.

VII.
I will not tell you
what these mean.
I am not coming
to your office again.
I carry my specific weight
but do not measure
the girth of ankle or waist.

Come visit me.
I will show you my new
flowers and birds.
I will let you ride
my white horse.

OBSERVATIONS

My back to the island,
I row across a surface I walked
two months ago when ice, unflawed,
so thick it blackened out of sight,
would pluck a deep boom
and I would pause, aware I slipped across
the back of a sleeping thing.
You were already gone by then,
living in unknown cities lurid with sun.

The mist this morning beads my arms.
Imagine this landscape and a woman
alone in a rowboat pausing at dawn
to watch the sinking moon.
I have a room that's big enough for sleep,
a bed that holds me and my book
until it tumbles out of hand.
The gulls are what I study now,
waking at night certain they skewer and shriek,
in every corner flapping their ragged wings.

I drag our old boat onto shale
in ways that you would scold.
The sentinels squawk and rise,
gray stone and gorse seethe with startled heads.
I go with my notebook, perch on my usual rock,
calm as a beekeeper up to the elbows.
I am braver than the woman you knew
and study only what I see.

July first, ten a.m.. They settle.
I watch a fledgling wander from its nest.
The mother is in flight to chase marauders,
then to wheel in pale blue.
The infant jerks its useless wings,
strays into another country
and is pecked to death by a mottled female.
Once it is down two young males strut and eat.
Ten thirty. The mother descends
to her empty nest. She preens.
I don't know if she cares.

JANITOR

He liked the cellar best.
To rise from floor to floor
was only to move into a clarity
of dirt. Sun showed streaks on windowpanes,
and snow threw back a light
that etched each cobweb on the ceiling.

He stooped and swiped,
left steps smoother every decade,
erased four children's crayon marks
then mopped the ashes of their cigarettes.
Still he kept his stool, old magazines
by the boiler where he could hear
water pressured into steam rising
while he leaned and dozed.

First he squinted and wore thick lenses.
His brushes missed the corners
of a house that was sifting down.
The nearest maples were puffs of shadow,
day was always on the verge of storm,
and someone who touched the windowsill
left a shocked splay of fingers all that year.

The last day Walter rose from underground
flinging himself blindly at the walls,
hands sweeping air to beat through layers of dark
the braille of newel post, risers,
shattering pane.

THE BATHER'S RITUAL

Each noon an old man limps to the beach.
Under his mantle he changes,
strips to a loincloth
so he can show his body
to the sky and arched horizon of sea.
He spreads his mat,
does not regard the other bathers
whose only desire is vanity of skin,
lies down with cruel rocks
lumped beneath him.

He turns to his side
and slowly lifts one arm
with counted precision of a dancer,
revolves again to raise the other
pitting vertebrae against the stones.
He does not wince, but waits for the moment
some god will open the portal of his body
and tread the threshold where his bones
dance to unlock their rusting tumblers.

The presence enters some antechamber,
shoulder, hips, or shin.
He limps down into waves,
borne on the salt cold drag
that lifts his weight.

A DREAM BEFORE SLEEP

Do you know how some houses
where you've spent years as a child
have shapes you keep on seeing?
So many of my dreams still happen there.
In the big attic we would lie on cots.
Miss Staples read *Kidnapped* again and again
but I didn't mind because I never heard it all.
When rain fell on the slates,
dripping onto windowsills, I'd doze.
She had a steady, quiet voice
I think of when I'm trying to sleep.

There was a boy named Nicky, hulking in his walk
and always poking a cheek with his tongue
or chewing on it when he worked at math.
We never knew how old he was.
He'd hurt himself when young,
fell off a bike, and he wasn't dumb
but his head worked poorly in some ways.
He loved recess and being *it* and showing
how fast and far he could run.
He'd take the small ones and make them all join hands
around the maple stump, and then he'd dance.
Oh, it was beautiful, though I didn't know it then,
like the house before it burned.

He was much bigger than us all,
bent double with one of our hands in each of his,
singing as we circled
then fell down.

THE WORK OF SAWS

She told me *Never mind*
and I left saplings
waist-high from the stump
we've got too little green.
They'd passed my shoulder
by the summer's end
were scraggled weeds
against the snow.
I cut one for no reason.
Our first child came
that spring, born
in the house, bawling
the leaves onto trees
and for ten years we lost
account of what it was up to
reaching toward the porch
lining the walls
with shadows in the night
as if four children
bent us inward
putting other worlds
far out of sight.
Once an owl clung
shivering through a day
blinked and rose above
our shouts, once our eldest
Josh went to the top
and sent his mother white
and trembling to pray him down
from an attic window--

grew through our dreams
and held them forked like nests
as one by one our flesh
dropped into their own lives,
watched as one who was pilot
came home bound in wood
risen beyond his mother's pleas,
until the sound its branches made
when we were sole possessors
of closed doors and floors walked
only by the pinch or flex of air
were our own breaths
our own stiff arch and rattle
in old winds.
It died like other elms
the neighbors take for firewood
split and burn.
Today she thought the saws
were airplanes on the lawn,
daft in a nightgown
her laughter made them pause.
I've had my stroke
my ears hum
and now they bring it down
limb by limb.

THE PERSISTENCE OF LIGHT

In spite of his brother's pleas
he runs home to be first
to arrive for dinner.
The present is unfinished,
a slight neglect from lack of screws
but Father's thanks are partial.
And when he sasses his mother
the old man's voice might be damning him
forever. Sent early to bed,
he hears his brother coddled
and vows eternal vengeance.

When walls and floors fall in
he wakes as if a voice has called,
but only the rush of crumbling, wave of darkness
dash over his startled body.
Sifting, a chock of brick on woods,
his brother's moans, and silence.

He waits for death
wondering how to tell its shape
but they break him upwards into light
and carry him rejoicing to a white place
where he is told no one else
in that house is living.

For years he survives the usual
waking in sweat, certain the rumble of trucks
is his house collapsing.
He is struck by guilt at every delay,
unable forever to please his father,
or stands for an hour watching his hand
tremble after it slaps his son,

fearing the world will stop again
before the recovering gestures of love.

But grass and trees, the altering shapes
of his woman's body persist
until the dream no longer revolves
but holds in its frame of grace
the scraping shovels, answering voice,
a sky that breaks new light across his face.

IMMIGRANTS

In the land where we first met
everyone spoke as we did
and I thought I understood.
The pasture we walked in tilted
toward a familiar sky. Our parents waited
in the town below. The cart was being repaired.
We could not decide our relationship.
I said cousin twice removed.

When they would not let us marry,
when I met you in the square at night
by the stone fountain long disconnected,
bearing all my life in what my hands could carry,
we did not question the future.
It moved always just ahead of us
serenely as that wide boat's prow.
We crowded in steerage, holding our tongues.

Understand, love, this is no complaint.
We all come to this country speaking different languages.
We learned how to talk by refusing
to say our own words even at home,
stumbling through dictionaries.
I came to love our wordless cries.
Our children spoke too fast for us to gather
more than half of what they said.

How simple the dream can be.
We turned down from that pasture

our eyes toward unbroken seas.
Bells, carried upward in the wind,
seemed gay. *We are dying, we are dying*
is my translation now, but only because I hear
                              them backwards.
We swerved into a grove of olives,
held up each other's bodies to the sun
and called them *love*.

You have fallen asleep in spite of pain.
It is dawn and habit wakes me
but the house is empty of chores.
I will my eyes to close.
We are walking on the opposite shore.
There is something at our feet as simple as stone
and I lift it, put it in your hand.
We can never stop naming the silence.

Carnegie-Mellon Poetry

1975
The Living and the Dead, Ann Hayes
In the Face of Descent, T. Alan Broughton

1976
The Week the Dirigible Came, Jay Meek
Full of Lust and Good Usage, Stephen Dunn

1977
*How I Escaped from the Labyrinth and
    Other Poems*, Philip Dacey
The Lady from the Dark Green Hills, Jim Hall
For Luck: Poems 1962-1977, H.L. Van Brunt
By the Wreckmaster's Cottage, Paula Rankin

1978
New & Selected Poems, James Bertolino
The Sun Fetcher, Michael Dennis Browne
A Circus of Needs, Stephen Dunn
The Crowd Inside, Elizabeth Libbey

1979
Paying Back the Sea, Philip Dow
Swimmer in the Rain, Robert Wallace
Far From Home, T. Alan Broughton
The Room Where Summer Ends, Peter Cooley
No Ordinary World, Mekeel McBride

1980
*And the Man Who Was Traveling Never Got
    Home*, H.L. Van Brunt
Drawing on the Walls, Jay Meek
The Yellow House on the Corner, Rita Dove
The 8-Step Grapevine, Dara Wier
The Mating Reflex, Jim Hall

1981
A Little Faith, John Skoyles
Augers, Paula Rankin
Walking Home from the Icehouse, Vern Rutsala
Work and Love, Stephen Dunn
The Rote Walker, Mark Jarman
Morocco Journal, Richard Harteis
Songs of a Returning Soul, Elizabeth Libbey

1982
The Granary, Kim R. Stafford
Calling the Dead, C.G. Hanzlicek